THE MYSTERY OF ATLANTIS

by Amy C. Rea

Dover Public Library
Dover, Delaware 19901
302-736-7030

Content Consultant
Kenneth L. Feder, PhD
Professor of Anthropology
Central Connecticut State University

Core Library

An Imprint of Abdo Publishing
abdopublishing.com

abdopublishing.com

Published by Abdo Publishing, a division of ABDO, PO Box 398166, Minneapolis, Minnesota 55439. Copyright © 2016 by Abdo Consulting Group, Inc. International copyrights reserved in all countries. No part of this book may be reproduced in any form without written permission from the publisher. Core Library™ is a trademark and logo of Abdo Publishing.

Printed in the United States of America, North Mankato, Minnesota
092015
012016

THIS BOOK CONTAINS
RECYCLED MATERIALS

Cover Photo: iStockphoto
Interior Photos: iStockphoto, 1, 7, 38; Géza Maróti, 4, 43; World History Archive/Newscom, 8 (top); Red Line Editorial, 8 (bottom), 29; Wikimedia Commons, 11, 12; William Scott-Elliott, 15, 45; Ignatius Donnelly/Library of Congress, 19; DK Images, 22; akg-images/Johann Brandstetter/Newscom, 24; akg-images/Newscom, 32; Bernd Weiëbrod/Picture-Alliance/DPA/AP Images, 35; NASA, 36

Editor: Mirella Miller
Series Designer: Ryan Gale

Library of Congress Control Number: 2015945990

Cataloging-in-Publication Data
Rea, Amy C.
 The mystery of Atlantis / Amy C. Rea.
  p. cm. -- (Mysteries of history)
 ISBN 978-1-68078-023-9 (lib. bdg.)
 Includes bibliographical references and index.
 1. Atlantis (Legendary place)--Juvenile literature.   I. Title.
 398.23--dc23

                                                                    2015945990

CONTENTS

CHAPTER ONE

ATLANTIS AND PLATO

What is Atlantis? Some might say it is a myth. Others say it is a true story. Either way, it is about a continent that was home to talented, educated, wealthy, and powerful people. But when the people became too powerful, they angered the Greek gods. The gods sent earthquakes and floods as punishment. Atlantis could not hold out against the storms and sank into the sea,

There have been many interpretations of what Atlantis looked like throughout the years.

never to be seen again. Many scientists have searched for evidence that Atlantis existed. Some believe they have found answers. Others believe those scientists are wrong.

Plato: Writer and Thinker

One thing we do know is that Plato is the source of the Atlantis story. A philosopher and teacher, Plato was born in Greece in 428 BCE. A philosopher is someone who studies and teaches about knowledge and truth. Plato is said to have had one of the greatest minds in history. Plato created a school, the Academy, in Athens, Greece.

Along with teaching, Plato wrote about many topics, including humans, justice, and truth. He explored what makes a good society. Plato also wrote dialogues. These were stories in which educated people would discuss different ideas about humanity. Two of his dialogues, *Timaeus* and *Critias*, mention Atlantis. In Plato's writing, the character Critias said

Plato's writings on many different subjects were popular philosophical teachings during his time.

Asia

N

What Plato Knew About Asia

Critias said Atlantis was an island bigger than Libya and Asia combined. For the ancient Greeks, "Libya" was the name of Africa. If you look on a map, you will see Asia is the largest continent on Earth. Plato may not have known how large Asia is. In his day, Libya might have seemed larger than Asia. Look at the map that shows how Plato viewed the world. Then look at the current map that shows Asia. How could those differences affect Atlantis's size according to Plato?

Atlantis was a true story handed down through generations of Greeks.

In the story, the Greek god Poseidon, who ruled the seas, created Atlantis. Poseidon married a human named Cleito. Poseidon wanted to keep Cleito safe, so he built a palace on Atlantis. The palace was on a mountain peak and was surrounded by stone walls. Poseidon also built a temple honoring himself.

Because Atlantis was an island, Atlanteans met many people from other countries as they sailed nearby. At first, these meetings were friendly. Then the Atlanteans became greedy. They wanted to take over other countries and people. Zeus, the ruler of the

PERSPECTIVES
How Big Was Atlantis?

Africa and Asia are two of the largest continents. Plato would not have known the exact size of these continents. They cover nearly two-thirds of the world. How could Atlantis be bigger than Asia and Africa yet disappear overnight? This is one reason some people do not believe Atlantis existed.

gods, punished the Atlanteans' greed with storms that sank the island approximately 11,000 years before modern times.

Allegory or History?

Some people believe Atlantis was a real place and want to find where the island disappeared. Others are convinced it was not real at all. Plato's writing is one reason some people doubt Atlantis was real. He often wrote allegories. An allegory is a story that is not necessarily true. It is meant to teach a lesson to the reader.

People who believe in Atlantis point out that the character Critias said Atlantis was a true story. Critias said the story was

Truth or Fiction?

Although Plato wrote many allegories, he often had characters in his stories say whether the stories were true. More than once in *Timaeus*, Critias noted when a story was not true or when he could not prove a story. At least three times in *Timaeus*, he said the story of Atlantis was an actual fact. Did Plato believe what he wrote about Critias? It is likely we will never know for sure.

A Latin translation of *Timaeus* from the 1400s

handed down to him through many people from Solon. Solon traveled to Egypt and heard the story from a priest. Solon was a real person. Is his story real too? If it is, why did no other writers during or before Plato's time write about it?

CHAPTER TWO

AN OCCULT WORLD

Plato introduced Atlantis to the world. It is still talked about centuries later. It even became a popular idea to people who believed in the paranormal or supernatural, which were referred to as the occult. People who study the occult are called occultists. Atlantis became a favorite story for many occultists in the late 1800s.

Madame Blavatsky came up with new theories surrounding Atlantis beginning in the late 1800s.

Madame Blavatsky

Madame Helena Blavatsky was an occultist and author who first wrote about Atlantis in 1877. She believed a war between the forces of good and evil destroyed Atlantis. The forces of evil took over the island and misused their magical powers, causing the disasters that ruined Atlantis.

Blavatsky believed in other things about Atlantis too. Scientists at the time were puzzled. They knew lemurs lived on the island of Madagascar, off the coast of Africa. They had also found lemur fossils in other parts of Africa and India. They did not know how this was possible. One idea was that a continent with several islands had once connected all of these places. It would have allowed lemurs to travel freely. Scientists called the continent Lemuria.

Madame Blavatsky said Atlantis and Lemuria might be the same place. She said this knowledge was given to her during a journey to Tibet. In her multivolume book *The Secret Doctrine,* she wrote that

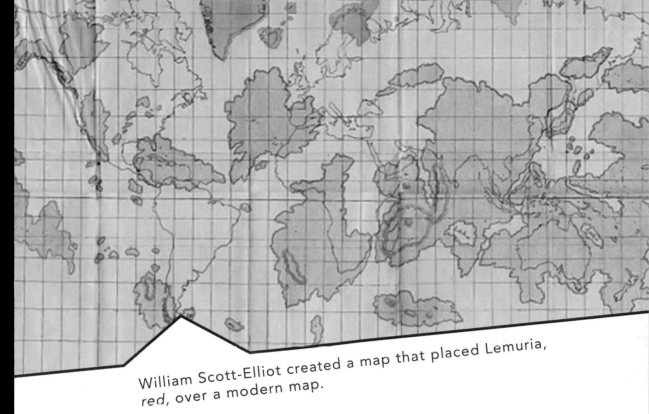

William Scott-Elliot created a map that placed Lemuria, *red*, over a modern map.

Tibetan sages had given her written records about Lemuria. These records indicated Lemuria was home to people who had four arms and eyes in the backs of their heads. Atlantis had people who were more similar to humans. Blavatsky wrote the Atlanteans were descendants of the ancient Lemurians. Their bodies had changed with time.

Other occultists added to her ideas. William Scott-Elliot wrote that he had learned of people from the planet Venus who had come to Earth and

Continental Drift

Many occultists believed a land bridge explained why lemurs were found in both Africa and India. There is no evidence that such a bridge ever existed in this region. However, a scientist named Alfred Wegener proposed a theory that explained the lemur question in 1912. It was called continental drift. His theory said that long ago, all continents were one large land mass called Pangaea. Pangaea broke apart into smaller continents. Later, some details of continental drift were disproved. Scientists found evidence for a new theory called plate tectonics. Continents are on large slabs of rock. These slabs move under the ocean floor, which can cause the continents to slowly move away from each other.

rearranged its landmasses. James Churchward said Lemuria was a landmass called Mu and Atlantis was a colony of Mu. Churchward said his source for this information was a tablet in an Indian monastery. Scott-Elliot and Churchward were followers of Blavatsky. They wanted to be part of the occultist movement as well.

The accounts of Lemuria and Mu have many problems. No evidence suggests a land bridge existed between Africa and India. Scientists have since discovered plate tectonics, a more likely explanation for how lemurs were found in both Africa and India. There are no records of people with four arms and eyes in the backs of their heads. There is also no trace of Madame Blavatsky's records from Tibet. In fact, there is no proof she ever went to Tibet.

Ignatius Donnelly

One of the first people to make Atlantis famous among occultists was Ignatius Donnelly. He was a politician and newspaper editor from Minnesota. Donnelly was interested in Atlantis. In 1882 he published a book called *Atlantis: The Antediluvian World. Antediluvian* means the time before the Biblical flood. In his book, Donnelly wrote his beliefs about Atlantis. He believed what Plato wrote was fact. Donnelly also believed Atlantis was the Garden of Eden. He saw Atlantis as the place where human civilization began. Donnelly said the gods and goddesses of Greek, Hindu, and Scandinavian mythology were based on stories created by the

Atlanteans. Donnelly believed Atlantis was destroyed by a natural disaster, not by angry gods.

Donnelly said Plato was telling the truth. However, he also said other proof besides Plato's writings proved Atlantis was real. Donnelly wrote that Egypt was once a colony of Atlantis. According to him, South American cultures and the Egyptians shared customs and parts of languages. The Egyptians mummified their dead. So did many South American cultures. The Egyptians built large pyramids, and so did people in Mexico. Donnelly said this proved Atlantis existed. He thought only one source could inspire things such as pyramids. If Atlantis were a large island between the two continents, it would be the source. Atlantis would have connected cultures on both sides of the Atlantic Ocean. Both Egyptians and Mexicans would have learned how to build such large structures from the Atlanteans.

Scientists have found that the Egyptian pyramids are almost 2,000 years older than the ones in Mexico.

Donnelly thought the Atlantean culture had spread across the Atlantic Ocean. This map shows in white where he believed similar cultures were found.

They learned this long after Donnelly wrote that the pyramids were built at the same time. Knowing that the pyramids were built so many years apart makes Donnelly's idea less believable.

There were other differences too. Egyptian mummies were prepared differently than mummies found in Mexico. Their languages were not as much alike as Donnelly thought. Donnelly's ideas have not held up as science has become more advanced. However, his ideas were strongly supported by other people who studied the occult.

Edgar Cayce

Edgar Cayce had new things to say about Atlantis in the 1920s. Cayce considered himself a spiritual healer. He would lie down and fall into a trance. While in a trance, he said he could talk about things he did not know about when he was awake. Sometimes he used this information to diagnose others who were ill. Cayce believed his trances also allowed him to see Atlantis and speak with Atlanteans. Based on what he saw, Cayce said, Atlantis was a very advanced civilization. The people had things such as airplanes, elevators, and even power from crystals. They were able to overpower gravity. This was helpful for building pyramids.

Cayce said former Atlanteans were reincarnating into Americans. He said the Atlanteans he spoke to during his trances told him about many things that would happen in the future. For example, California would fall into the sea. He also said Atlantis would rise up from the sea

PERSPECTIVES
Atlantean Technology

Cayce believed Atlanteans had advanced technology, including airplanes, radio, submarines, and explosives. As technology became more innovative, the Atlanteans used these tools in destructive ways. Eventually, these tools led to the ruin of the city. Cayce said advancing technology could cause the same destruction to happen again. Cayce was right that technology became much more advanced in the 1900s, but it did not destroy an entire continent.

Cayce believed Atlantis had highly advanced and intelligent citizens capable of building a large city.

in 1968 or 1969. Cayce predicted the East Coast, including New York City, was going to slip into the sea and be destroyed at this time.

The problem with Cayce's information is that so little can be proven. And many of his predictions did not occur. No evidence proves this advanced civilization ever existed. Cayce could not prove Atlanteans were talking to him. Many people during the early 1900s pretended to receive information from spirits. They often were proven wrong. Was Cayce one of them? It seems likely, because Atlantis did not reappear and California and the East Coast have not fallen into the sea. These are likely tales Cayce told to earn attention from the public.

ATLANTIS'S LOCATION

If Atlantis is real, where is it? People who believe Atlantis exists want to find its location. Each group of people has its own ideas about where to look. These groups have looked across the globe in search of the lost city.

Plato said Atlantis was west of the Pillars of Hercules in the Atlantic Ocean. Today the Pillars of Hercules are called the Strait of Gibraltar. This

Many people believe that if Atlantis is real, it will be found underwater.

Mid-Atlantic Ridge

The Mid-Atlantic Ridge is a giant mountain range. It is 10,000 miles (16,000 km) long. It runs from the Arctic Ocean to the southern part of Africa. At some points, it is 1,000 miles (1,600 km) wide. The Mid-Atlantic Ridge moves about one-half to four inches (1.3–10 cm) each year. This is due to plate tectonics and seafloor spreading. Seafloor spreading is what happens when Earth's tectonic plates split apart and move away from each other.

narrow waterway is between Spain and Morocco. It connects the Mediterranean Sea to the Atlantic Ocean. In this area is a series of small islands called the Azores. The Azores were part of the Mid-Atlantic Ridge of underwater mountains. The underwater mountains were discovered in Donnelly's day. He believed the Azores were the last parts of Atlantis to remain above water. His theory suggested the Azores were going to sink with the rest of Atlantis.

The Mid-Atlantic Ridge was not sinking. In fact, it results from plate tectonics causing underwater mountains to grow, not sink. If Donnelly were correct, explorers should have found evidence of Atlantis around these underwater mountains. There would also be very little sediment on the ocean floor in that location. Instead, there are layers of sediment almost one-half of a mile (0.8 km) deep. It took millions of years for that sediment to build up. There is no evidence of a large island crashing to the ocean floor during those millions of years.

Beyond the Strait of Gibraltar

There have been many other theories about Atlantis's location. A Swedish professor named Olof Rudbeck published the first volume of a series called *Atlantica* in 1657. In it, he wrote that Sweden was actually Atlantis. Rudbeck used old Swedish folktales and mythology as part of his evidence. While trying to solve the mystery of Atlantis, Rudbeck helped make an important scientific discovery. He realized Earth was made of layers that built up with time. When he found old relics, he could date them based on the layer in which they were found. When he found several ancient burial mounds, he was sure they were from Atlantis. However, they were not from the right period. In spite of that, Rudbeck believed Sweden was Atlantis. A passage goes between Sweden and Denmark. Rudbeck said this was the Pillars of Hercules, not the Strait of Gibraltar. Many scholars did not agree.

A French astronomer named Jean-Sylvain Bailly began writing about Atlantis in 1775. He believed it was farther north, above the Arctic Circle. From there,

PERSPECTIVES
Spain

In 2011 Richard Freund, a professor in the United States, used deep-ground radar, digital mapping, and satellite imagery to explore the southern coast of Spain. He believes Atlantis is there because of evidence from a stone slab that may have been part of Atlantis. He also saw squares and rectangles in the ground that may have been former buildings. However, Spanish researchers do not agree with Freund. They have reported that their work shows Freund's findings date from approximately 711 to 1250 CE. Atlantis would be much older than that.

Where Did Plato Think Atlantis Was?

Many scholars think Plato believed Atlantis was in the Atlantic Ocean, directly west of the Strait of Gibraltar. Many others think that is wrong. Look at the locations marked on the map. If Plato lived in Greece, which places seem most likely for Atlantis's location? Which ones seem least likely? Why?

Atlanteans could have migrated. If Atlantis were an advanced civilization, they would have spread their knowledge.

Others did not agree. In the 1800s, many theories were published. Atlantis was said to be in places such as Iran, Nigeria, the Netherlands, and Malta. In the early 1900s, Brazil, the United Kingdom,

North America, and Egypt were named as possible locations of Atlantis. Some people said Atlantis had not sunk but had become an African desert.

These hypotheses are all hard to prove. If Atlantis had truly disappeared during a natural disaster, there should be evidence in the Earth's layers. There should also be evidence in nearby communities. If an island that large sank rapidly, it would likely have caused a tsunami. There is no evidence of a tsunami during that time.

FURTHER EVIDENCE

Chapter Three covers various ideas about where Atlantis might be. What is one of the main points of this chapter? What key evidence supports this point? Read the article at the website below. Find a quote on this website that supports the main point you identified. Does the quote support an existing piece of evidence in this chapter? Or does it offer a new piece of evidence?

Lost City of Atlantis
mycorelibrary.com/atlantis

Many people claim they have read Plato and understand where Atlantis is based on his writings. Writer and skeptic Benjamin Radford says this:

> Many people over the centuries have . . . speculated about where Atlantis would be found. Countless Atlantis "experts" have located the lost continent all around the world, based on the same set of facts. . . .
>
> Plato, however, is crystal clear about where his Atlantis is: "For the ocean there was at that time navigable; for in front of the mouth which you Greeks call, as you say, 'the pillars of Heracles,' [Hercules] there lay an island which was larger than Libya and Asia together." In other words, it lies in the Atlantic Ocean beyond "the pillars of Hercules" [Strait of Gibraltar]. Yet it has never been found in the Atlantic, or anywhere else.

> Source: Benjamin Radford. "'Lost' City of Atlantis: Fact & Fable." Live Science. Live Science, October 31, 2014. Web. Accessed June 16, 2015.

Point of View
The writer has a strong opinion about the many proposed locations of Atlantis. What is his opinion? Do you agree? Why or why not?

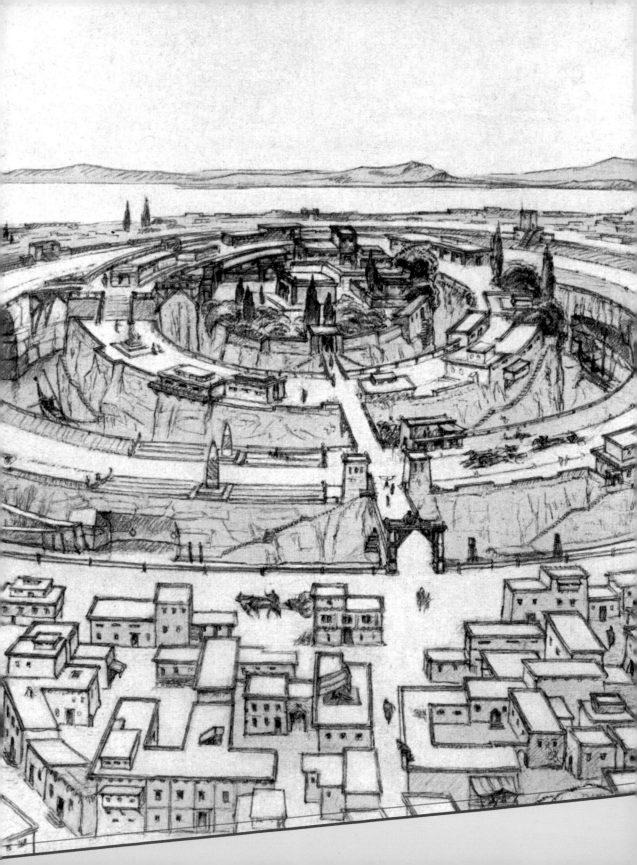

IS THE ANSWER IN GREECE?

Another theory says Atlantis was actually the Greek island of Crete. The Minoan Empire lived there from approximately 2000 BCE to 1500 BCE. Archaeologists have uncovered many pieces of the Minoan Empire. These discoveries show the empire was an advanced civilization. Grand palaces have been excavated. They contain complex designs, pottery, and metalwork. There is

This illustration by Walter Heiland shows the center of Atlantis as it would appear if the lost city were found on the island of Crete.

evidence the Minoans set up trade routes along the Mediterranean Sea to places such as Egypt and what is now Turkey. There were laws that made women equal to men. Archaeologists have also found written documents, but scholars have not yet been able to translate them.

Many scientists believe that sometime around 1500 BCE, the Minoans seem to have disappeared. Other scientists say it happened later than 1500 BCE. That would mean it was not the right period for Atlantis. If it were around 1500 BCE, the destruction sounds similar to Atlantis. All but one of the Minoan grand palaces were burned. The towns in the southern and eastern parts of the island were badly damaged. Crete is in an area prone to earthquakes. The palaces and other buildings have evidence of damage from various earthquakes. Yet the people survived previous natural disasters.

Archaeologists have found extravagant buildings and temples where the Minoan Empire once stood.

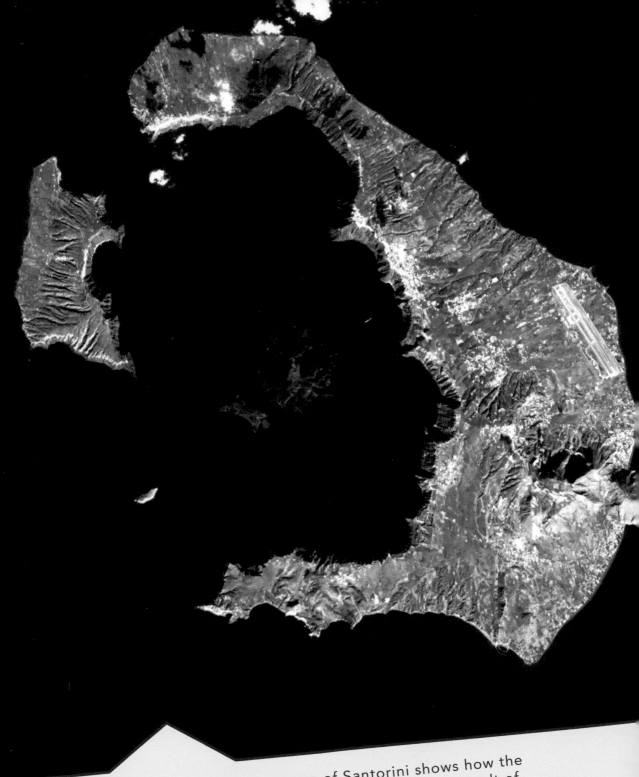

This NASA satellite image of Santorini shows how the island has broken into smaller islands as the result of earthquakes over thousands of years.

What Happened to the Minoan Empire?

The island of Santorini was 80 miles (130 km) north of Crete. Between 1640 and 1600 BCE, there was a massive volcanic eruption on Santorini. The eruption was so strong it broke Santorini into several smaller islands. Scientists believe an eruption of that size would have sent a large tsunami to Crete. The tsunami could have sent a wave of water one-half of a mile (0.8 km) high into the island. This

PERSPECTIVES
Santorini as Atlantis

Some people think Santorini was Atlantis, not Crete. This makes sense because a volcanic eruption blew the island apart. Plato wrote that Atlantis had moats with a canal leading to the sea. This would be possible only if the island were mostly flat. Santorini has mountains and volcanoes. It is also a very small island, not nearly as large as Critias described. There is evidence of homes and of people living on Santorini in the past, but no bodies or signs of wealth have ever been found. The volcanic eruption may have started as a series of earthquakes. The people on Santorini may have left the area before the eruption. This does not fit the Atlantis story.

Some believe Crete is where Atlantis will one day be found.

would have destroyed buildings and ships and killed many people.

It is not hard to see why many people think Crete is Atlantis. However, some things about Crete do not match Critias's story from Plato's dialogue. The tsunami took place more than 8,000 years later than he said Atlantis sank. Some scholars believe the source for Critias's story used a written character for *thousand* when they meant *hundred*. If that is true, the timing of the tsunami arriving at Crete is right.

Plato described Atlantis's geography in great detail. He said moats were connected to the sea by a canal. There is no evidence of that on Crete. The location is also a problem. Critias stated Atlantis was near the Pillars of Hercules, or the Strait of Gibraltar. Crete is far away from that area. In addition, Crete is still an island above water. Critias made it clear Atlantis sank. Critias said there were tame elephants on Atlantis. But there is no evidence of elephants on Crete when the Minoan Empire existed.

Rewriting History

It is possible Plato heard the story of the volcanic eruption and the damage on Santorini and Crete. He might have been inspired to use some of those facts to create a story that was not all true. Many writers have written stories that are mostly fiction but based on fact. Plato's dialogues could be among them.

Fact or Fiction?

There are many hypotheses about Atlantis. None of them can be completely proven. Many scientists believe Atlantis is a myth. They say it is a story Plato created as a starting point to talk about other topics. In Plato's story, one of the characters says Atlantis is real.

Unless scientists discover proof that matches Plato's story exactly, it is likely the mystery of Atlantis will never be solved. Some people say Atlantis does not exist because nobody has solved the mystery. But others say Atlantis is still waiting to be discovered. Only time will tell who is right.

EXPLORE ONLINE

Chapter Four talks about how the Greek island of Crete may be Atlantis. The article at the website below goes into more detail about this theory. How does the information on the website compare with the information in Chapter Four? What new information did you learn from the website?

The Fall of the Minoans

mycorelibrary.com/atlantis

Why was Plato the only person who wrote about Atlantis? Author J. Allan Danelek discusses this in his book *Atlantis: Lessons from the Lost Continent:*

> *Are we to really believe that such an important historical event—a vast war that engaged all the nations of the known world in a powerful life-or-death struggle and ended in a catastrophe that obliterated an entire race—could have been overlooked by a host of other writers for thousands of years? While I recognize that a huge body of literature was lost over the centuries to fires and various mindless acts of destruction, I still find it suspicious that Plato's account was and remains the first and last word on the subject.*

Source: J. Allan Danelek. Atlantis: Lessons from the Lost Continent. *Woodbury, MN: Llewellyn, 2008. Print. 35.*

Changing Minds

Imagine you believe Atlantis is real. Your best friend has the opposite opinion. Write a short essay trying to change your friend's mind. Make sure you explain your opinion. Include facts and details that support your reasons.

Plato told the true story of Atlantis.

Evidence for:

- In the dialogues, Critias said it was a true story.

Evidence against:

- No other ancient writers wrote about Atlantis.

Atlantis was an island in the Atlantic Ocean, near the Strait of Gibraltar.

Evidence for:

- Critias said Atlantis was located near the Pillars of Hercules, which are known to be the Strait of Gibraltar.

Evidence against:

- There is no sign of a large island having sunk in that area.

Atlantis is actually Sweden.

Evidence for:

- There are old legends that match stories of Atlantis.

Evidence against:

- There is no sign of a civilization being in Sweden at that time.

Atlantis was the island of Crete.

Evidence for:

- There was an advanced civilization on Crete that disappeared after a tsunami.

Evidence against:

- Crete is not near the Pillars of Hercules and did not sink.

STOP AND THINK

Tell the Tale

Chapter Four of this book discusses the island of Crete and the tsunami that devastated it. Imagine you are living on the island of Crete at that time. Write 200 words about hearing the volcano erupt on Santorini and seeing the tsunami coming. How would you feel? What would you do?

You Are There

This book talks about the different locations where Atlantis might be found. Choose one and imagine you are traveling there when it was still above the ocean. Write a letter home telling your friends what you have found. What do you notice about your surroundings? Are you on an island? Are you close to any well-known landmarks? Be sure to add plenty of details to your notes.

Surprise Me

Chapter Two talks about different occult theories of Atlantis. After reading this book, what two or three theories about Atlantis did you find most surprising? Write a few sentences about each theory. Why did you find each one surprising?

Dig Deeper

After reading this book, what questions do you still have about Atlantis? With an adult's help, find a few reliable sources that can help answer your questions. Write a paragraph about what you learned.

GLOSSARY

allegory
a story with a hidden meaning, usually moral or political

archaeologists
scientists who study bones and tools of ancient people to learn about their lives and activities

fossil
the preserved remains of plants and animals from the distant past

monastery
a place where religious people live and work together

mythology
the stories or beliefs of a culture or society

occult
things that are believed in but are not easily proven or seen

philosopher
a person who studies things such as knowledge, truth, and the meaning of life

reincarnation
the belief that when a person dies, his or her soul goes into another human body

strait
a narrow passageway connecting two bodies of water

trance
a sleeplike state

LEARN MORE

Books

Karst, Ken. *Atlantis.* Mankato, MN: Creative
    Education, 2015.

Owings, Lisa. *Atlantis.* Minneapolis, MN: Bellwether
    Media, 2015.

Walker, Kathryn. *The Mystery of Atlantis.* New York:
    Crabtree, 2010.

Websites

To learn more about Mysteries of History, visit
booklinks.abdopublishing.com. These links are
routinely monitored and updated to provide the most
current information available.

Visit **mycorelibrary.com** for free additional tools for
teachers and students.

INDEX

ABOUT THE AUTHOR

Amy C. Rea is a writer from Minnesota. She loves to read, write, and hang out with her kids and dog. She has always been fascinated by stories about unsolved mysteries.